Open to Currents

Open to Currents

Kenneth Sherman

Wolsak and Wynn . Toronto

Acknowledgements are made to the editors of the following magazines where some of these poems first appeared: *ARC*, *Canadian Literature*, *The Dalhousie Review*, *Descant*, *Grain*, *The Idler*, *Palaver*, *Parchment*, *Poetry Canada Review*, *Viewpoints*.

Typeset in Bookman, printed in Canada by
The Coach House Press, Toronto.

I wish to thank Samiha Abdel Sayed for her insightful comments that helped with my Baudelaire translation. Two lines from my sonnet, "Florence, 1973", owe their origin to Mary McCarthy's *The Stones of Florence*.

Author's photo by Marie Sherman.

The publishers gratefully acknowledge support by
The Canada Council and The Ontario Arts Council.

Wolsak and Wynn Publishers Ltd.
Don Mills Post Office Box 316
Don Mills, Ontario, Canada, M3C 2S7

Canadian Cataloguing in Publication Data
Kenneth Sherman, 1950-
Open to Currents
Poems.
ISBN 0-919897-29-0
I. Title.
PS8587.H37063 1992 C811'.52 C92-094094-3
PR9199.3.S43063 1992

For Peter Wood, Ruth Theohar, Art Spence,
and George Gillanders - the teachers.

Contents

PART I

Seminal cloth 11
Currents 12
Visiting Eli Mandel 14
Travelling carnival 17
Fedora 21
Yasur 23
Inscription 24
Dogs 26
Eternal return 27
Earth movers 28
The non-country 30
At the Dyer Memorial 32
Talking it through 34

PART II

Justine's ballet class 39
The water skier 40
Sieve 41
The eschatology of bees 42
Fish cart 44
Hallowe'en pumpkin 46
The owls 47
Fat black bird 48
Chair 50
A black book 52
Treasure of the Sierra Madre 54
Two poems inspired by the prints of George Raab 55

PART III

Mahabalipuram: Dravidian ruins 59
What you see when you enter Beijing's
Museum of the Revolution 61
Poland 62
The village 63
The cemetery 65
Warsaw 66
Cities 67
1. Paris, 1969 67
2. Venice 68
3. Florence 69
4. Chiangmai 70
5. Xian 71
6. Saigon, 1973 72
7. Akko 73
8. Jerusalem 74
9. Hiroshima 75
10. Kyoto 76
11. Madras 77
12. Agra 78
13. Benares 79
14. Bombay 80
15. Kandy 81
16. Colombo 82
17. Kiev, 1988 83
18. Leningrad, 1988 84
19. Halifax 85
20. Toronto 86

I

SEMINAL CLOTH

In my father's tailor shop
men sewed arms to shoulders,
measured legs as the day drained
to where razors and pins shone in the dimness.
I could hear the flesh-like tearing of thread.

In the box beneath the cutting-table
the material scraps gathered:
sharkskin, hounds-tooth,
herringbone tweed.

As a child, I buried myself in that darkness
beneath the marvellous patterns
and practised the animal names
until the box became a boat,
the darkness, a sea.

Far off, I could hear
the muffled voice of my father, calling.

CURRENTS

Turn of the century.
He shovelled snow for the city
far from his impoverished Poland
or from any imagined Jerusalem.

Then the sweatshops
and the machine-gun staccato
of sewing machines that made a mockery
of the nomenclature *Singer*.

His eyes grew hard as buttons.
His children's hunger bound him
like needle-tugged thread.
I loved the smell of cloth

in the shop he later bought
and the old furnace
and his breath sometimes redolent
of *Seagram & Sons*,

his mixture of anger and humour
knowing that his hands and making couldn't last
now that there were "suits off the rack,"
monotony walking in identical lapels.

A sceptic's scowl,
a forehead
creased like a page
from a book of the perplexed

folded for reference
in my memory,
that inheritance
open to currents.

VISITING ELI MANDEL

i

Some things are truly hard.
Seeing you like this
at the Castleview Home for the Aged,
colourless, eyes vacant

and those other pale shades
that hover about us. Is this
what Coleridge meant
by his Life-In-Death?

I wished to make more
of what they related:
your hurling food,
tearing off your shirt

bearing down to the elemental
like Blake's Ezekiel,
but no,
as the orderly reminded:

"these small aggressions
of the stroke victim."

ii

What should remain unsaid?
When I spoke your name
you put your hand up
as to cover your face
and I thought you were embarrassed
that I should see you, shirtless
skeleton without language,
though the nurse assured
you were beyond such caution.

And ought I be embarrassed to write this?
How much of the real, Eli,
do we let in: the sour smell
of the institution, your one good arm
darting out to grasp the dark railing:
was that the desperation
I found so attractive
in your poems
or blind reflex?

iii

I swallow these images
and go back in time
to your sharp comments
on my manuscripts

your eyes flashing over the text,
displaced scribe of Kiev,
always leading me, the slow student,
into the unexpected perspective,

then, and strangely now,
now with this greatest of all puzzles
as I sit and talk to you
or to your silent presence

and make
my connection.

TRAVELLING CARNIVAL

i

As a young teenager
I worked one summer for a travelling carnival.
The concessions were owned by a man named
Fagan who was more evil
than the character in Dickens.
Bald, with a thin upper body that bulged
into an enormous waist, he was the shape
of a giant egg, or one of those toddler's toys
that when you hit goes down
and swivels back up again.
He often came to inspect
with two thugs who wore suits and sunglasses
and never talked.

ii

I had two jobs.
One was selling balloons
that you punch holding a long rubber band.
They were filled with sand
and made the sound of a medicine man's rattle.
My other job was operating the Ferris wheel.

iii

One night at closing time, Fagan arrived
with two whores from Toronto. He gave me five bucks,
told me to send him and the women to the top,
stop the machine and get lost for half an hour.
I could hear their laughter as I left the darkened lot
and walked down to the pebble shore of the lake
just beyond the small town we were playing.
It was then I discovered that water coming in
sounds like water — not sighs, not the sobbing of tears.
I stood watching the lights blinking on the opposite
shore, imagining there was someone there alone
staring out through the darkness
about to set out on a journey.

iv

The guy I worked with and learned from was Bucky Harris:
about 5 ft. tall, close to sixty, he had cauliflower ears
and a voice like Wallace Beery. He'd been a professional
wrestler and an infantryman in the second world war.
"Kid," he'd say,
"I killed more krauts than you have hair on your ass.
And those British broads — all they wanted
was beer and meat if you know what I mean."

v

We shared a trailer.
Each night Bucky woke up shuddering
from bad dreams. "It's nothing, kid," he'd say.
"Go back to sleep."
Long after he'd gone back to snoring
I'd lie in the dark and stare at the low mildewed
ceiling as the trailer grew more and more narrow
until it seemed no wider or deeper
than a box.

vi

The highlight of that summer
was falling in love with Nadine.
She worked for the Dairy Queen,
had golden hair, wore a polka dot bow tie,
white shirt, white pants and red suspenders.
We'd talk and talk. I took her out in a
rowboat and told her
I wanted to be a poet.
When I told Bucky about her he laughed
and asked if I'd got inside her pants.
I recall her hand trailing in the wake
behind the boat, her face even more intimidatingly
gorgeous in the dusk
and the starry glint of her earrings.
Lost possibilities.

vii

For some reason I've begun to see him more clearly,
that solitary boy
in the faded blue jean jacket
who'd help the smiling couples into their silver carriages,
press down the giant lever
and watch the great wheel turn.
As I grow older,
he grows younger, more innocent.
And I feel anxious about him
as a father might feel about a son
who has decided to travel.
I want to hold him to me, advise him
how to speak to the cynical,
the broken. I want to slip this very poem
into his pocket for an amulet, a charm,
but he's so far away

though travelling toward me
like that other I once imagined
setting out from
some dark, some distant shore.

FEDORA

On a downtown street corner
near Tip Top Tailors
I find myself
looking for my father.

I pass a darkened hat shop
south on Spadina
that displays a fedora —
the sort he used to wear

in the dead heart of winter
when he'd come home from work
drained, without words.
In the sudden warmth of the house

his glasses fog.
He takes off his coat and his hat
then pours himself
a thimble of Scotch.

Under the bald glare
of a suburban streetlight
our driveway is filling
with snow.

My father eats his late supper
then again puts on
his hat and his coat.
My pillow is next

to my bedroom window
so I can hear
the clear and solitary
scrape of his shovel.

The sound slices through me.
What is he shovelling
if not the days
that lie buried

in the banks of whiteness
that will melt
or be carried by wind.
On a closet shelf,

years later, I find
my father's fedora
with its stained sweatband,
the possibility of its soft folds,

its rigid brim.
When I run my hand inside
along the cool satin lining
I can feel the absence.

Somewhere, my father is travelling
with what he could not give.
What he gave
I hold now in my hand.

YASUR

A shiny black scorpion
crawled from under a boulder
in the peach orchards of Yasur.
In the mauve pastel light of 5 a.m.
it did not startle me.
I worked silently between the green branches,
handling the flushed peaches.
I still recall how to pick them,
not pulling, but gently twisting the stem,
the blue plastic bucket
I placed them in,
my ladder only so high
so I'd strain to reach
what was sometimes out of reach,
my sneakers soaked through with dew.
The sun coming up was a severed
blood orange. Rising higher
it turned to white fire.
I worked until my head grew hazy
and I had to leave off picking
and climb down to rest
in the shade
near the half-filled wagon.

The last thing I recall
was the fruit's overpowering fragrance.
Then how to account
for that dark fragment
darting across the landscape of my dream
with its backward glance?

INSCRIPTION

In the peach orchards of Yasur
I met Hana,
the only child of survivors
born in the woods beyond Bergen-Belsen.

She gave me a copy of Amichai's poems
with a blue Mediterranean cover
and dark, Hebrew letters
that talk of the wounded chest as the door

to God's apartment. In another,
the poet writes his lover's name in the sand.
Hana wrote hers in the flyleaf
saying simply "from your summer companion,"

while I left her my copy
of *Portrait of the Artist as a Young Man*
and with an affected flourish quoted Rilke's
"love consists in this ..."

myself not knowing what love is.
A lifetime to be honest,
to bend the green branch
while she offered a season's gift,

the ooze of flushed peaches
and sweet sticky fingers
all brought back now by the cream page
with her spray of blue letters.

It was she who was the artist,
turning her parents' darkness
into a seizing of the moment,
taking the precious day for what it is,

sending me off in the direction
of this late revision,
this belated inscription
from a summer friend.

DOGS

I laboured there one summer
making red hots, wieners and those
named after a German town that begins with F
and whose prefix, in English, means candid.

No one dealt in the larynx of language.
Silence in the dyeing room
where, looped on racks, they bathed
in the eerie shade of infrared lamps.

Engineers in chalky lab coats
moved amongst them like spectres,
speechless hard hats, grim-lipped,
jotting on clipboards.

In the room where I worked the machinery was deafening,
our ears stuffed with cotton batting.
An arctic each morning where you'd see your breath;
a Sahara by noon. The body rioted.

Long hours, slim wages. Was I provider
or reaper, sending them down the conveyor,
slimy, intestinal,
thinking it strange they should resemble

that part of the body to which they were headed
like in some Pharaoh's dream
of sludge and kine
and flesh devouring flesh.

ETERNAL RETURN

I recall you walking on the campus green:
and the warm September breeze
pressed like a caress
to shape a body of your cotton dress.
That image was married to the past.

It came alive last Friday
as I walked from Lecture Hall A
and saw another moving dreamily
across the green campus sea —
a girl so beautiful and half my age.

I am not a sentimentalist,
nor do I go for the impossible wish:
her smile hurled me twenty years back,
dread sunk through me like a weighted sack —
the years, her smile, whatever cannot be grasped.

EARTH MOVERS

One summer I worked at my uncle's tire factory
watching an endless stream of shiny black tires
roll onto transport trucks. To my uncle,
they appeared as impressive zeros
strung out after a dollar sign and digit.
Some were the height of an African elephant
and were used on mining machines
called *earth movers*. My uncle's salesman,
John Hoffmayer, would drive a black Toronado
into northern Quebec to sell them to mining executives
who sat in prefab heated cabins,
dressed in cardigans, sipped warm rum
and told jokes about women.

I myself learned to load the monster tires.
As long as you kept them moving
you were o.k. In motion they could be balanced
which to me seemed indicative of the system.
If you stopped to consider them
they would topple over, threatening
to crush you to death.

All that summer, the sky
looked grey through the dusty skylight
of my uncle's factory, the men's flesh
pale and drained
against their sombre blue overalls.
We were making tires
for machines that would snort, whine
and claw deep into the earth's belly

while our days were rolling
my summer days
passing one after the other
out of the great circular moulds
with the monotony of black, shiny zeros.

THE NON-COUNTRY

It is double, wide
and flagrant with potential
yet something frigid
                                        and hard to move
at the core.

I have never seen the Rockies
but hear their grandeur
is almost impossible to bear.

A landscape of spaces.
Has the void
clogged our voices,
                                        shadowed us
like the God-lonely arctic light
in a Lauren Harris painting?

What of those stories of communes, settlers,
victories of exiles, why have we not
carried the myth of their hardness,
with a resoluteness
that silently bonds?

It is good to be free
of rousing anthems,
the flapping stripes,
prison of rhetoric,
those helmeted warriors
south of the border.
Still they carry their black beard
and blanched beast of a moral vision
for good or ill
while we peer into our respective
navels: the ontological disposition.

We are a mixture
that will not blend,
                                        so doubled forever,
possibly poetic.

If only we could see this as the right difference,
the new land
that is always out of reach,
changing,

and make a celebration
of our becoming.

AT THE DYER MEMORIAL

Just outside of Huntsville
down a dirt road,
dust clouds and the ricochet of stones
against our blue Ford's underbelly.

You pass two miles of dense bush
until suddenly you're at cut grass,
a clearing with stone benches,
the indigenous plants of Northern Ontario
labelled.

A planned pond
so thick with frogs
that when Adam stretches out his hand,
voilà —
          bulging Peter Lorre eyes
stare out of his small palm,
a white vinyl throat throbbing.

The security of the place
is open space, pure sun, visibility.

With dusk we decide to leave,
forms blurring, shifting into one another.
We hold hands on the path to the car
and pass the monument Mr. Dyer built
to preserve the name of his wife
who would no longer share with him
their green Algonquin summers,
his very name holding dying
or the dye of dusk seeping over us
but also the dyer's hand
and its wish for permanence.

Night descends so quickly
we end up walking more by feeling
than by sight.

How tender, the small fear
in our voices
as I fumble with the keys.

TALKING IT THROUGH

How long have we talked?

Years.

Your plants never wept
when I spoke of my problems.

Something has grown so light,
a pearl-grey feather, the vast
inner absence
diminished
by all the dialogues,
that gradual focus
and your sane face
poised
across the earth brown rug.

I think of you
as the blessed proctor of patience.

Workday afternoons,
sun piercing through blinds,
at times a distant city siren
broke through my personal
drama, and every other step
a crisis, so I asked, Do others live like this?

I open a velvet bag marked Seagram and Sons
to discover hurt relics,
shocked to realize they've grown old
but vivid as the child's quick hand
that placed them there.

Strange to come to control
by letting go.
                I go back into the fray
that is everyman's life,
resolute bedouin in the stretch
of his own inner scape,
sustained by those deep wadis of loss.

II

JUSTINE'S BALLET CLASS

In pink tights and black leotards
they resemble licorice all-sorts.
Each has her hair gathered in a disciplined bun.

If there is radiance, it is here,
reflected in these working mirrors
and shining hardwood floors,

these young forms
propelled by the leaping half-notes of Chopin
and by relentless Ena

exiled Russian ballerina:
"Nyo, nyot like zjat," she corrects
and bends,

her Leningrad calves
prominent from dance and bread lineups
spring a seamless pirouette.

Each girl is a tentative glass figure
on tiptoe, arms a taut bow
above the head

as she waits her turn
and takes off — astonished
to embrace mere air.

THE WATER-SKIER

Now he's cutting deep, his sun-burst slalom
splicing the wake, his life-jacketed torso
almost parallel to the reflective surface

his ear six astonished inches from water;
then swings back, enveloped
in a curtain of spray

biceps flexed, calves prominent,
circling the circuit's buoys
with the fluidity of a motion

that weaves back against itself,
a progressive S, heuristic script,
making a precision

of the engine's screaming revolutions,
his joy the sheer doing of it,
defying the lake that breaks and gasps

knowing in the end
it will swallow his presence,
his ever-having-been

returning to numb silence
after his yelp of accomplishment,
cold and glacial and still.

SIEVE

What passes through it
is always more than air.
Fluid of our lives, a moment's density
that weighs upon the handle
then pours down the sink like a prayer —

panic in the pipes,
a running anxiety
under the pitch
of the metropolis.

Once the earth was a sieve —
what passed through it
nourished.

In the night sky, that colander
of stars, those punctures of darkness,
implosion of black gas,
what the texts term "dark matter"

drawing you into curved air,
an endless returning
where your hands are shining, fluorescent
like the pale limbs of amphibians
or fetal creatures, potential,
there.

THE ESCHATOLOGY OF BEES

The striped prisoner's uniform
of bees,
            their monotony, their industry,
the terror of their hives.

Whose life do they live there,
with the others?
Their frenetic sound, electrical,
like some transformer
taken to its limit

though too profound for that.

They swarm in clouds,
jittery, atomic
about the brooding branches
of the tree.
Their layered homes
look shaggy, woven,
almost biblical.

Is it their hum,
their drone of lamentation
that has me focus on my shadow
frozen
on the gravel road?

I razor the combs
and raise the structured cells
to my lips

knowing what they make is sweet
though they speak
of final things.

FISH CART

In the market-square I saw the fish cart,
tilted, its old wood worn
into the malleable grey of clay.

The damp burlap was pulled back
revealing bass in tight fraternity,
a dumb chorus-line

a row of bloated tongues
laid out on chunks of hacked
and jagged ice.

Their flesh, which once touched
the numb, ear-splitting depths,
was a blue-black iridescence

behind the sheen of scales,
their fins fluted back like collapsed sails
after a star-back journey,

their cold white bellies
were flecked with traces
of the distant ritual gold.

And I knew they'd reached their destination
for each mouth was an astonished O
that had gorged on some truth

each metallic eye
seemed locked
on a relentless absolute

while above them, the clamour
of barter — shirts, skirts, flowers —
the spray of colours

pulsing in the midday air.

HALLOWE'EN PUMPKIN

I brought it to decompose
by the fence in our backyard garden
and watched it rot through foul November,
its deepening orange, a molten, setting sun.

For weeks it held the shock of human expression
amongst the ordinary sparrows and squirrels
with its mouth's round note of astonishment
and its star-shaped eyes, charred and mournful.

The stem from its head
which had served as a handle to open
that night of candles and masks
had withered into the dry worm of a question.

Its dark absence of ears
now led to a riddling where.
And I could see into its future
all blanketed by white powder

gradually greeting the compost of April,
ready for our birth garden
though what it would bring forth
would be beauty, not invention.

And peering into its hollow spaces
I recalled the quick eyes of the children
that night by the harvest table,
the determined lines they sketched on flesh.

THE OWLS
(from Baudelaire)

In the shelter of yews, dark as slate,
the owls arrange themselves in lines.
Like alien gods their eyes
flash red. They meditate.

Without the slightest stir they'll hold
until the saddest hour
when the sun relinquishes power
and darkness unfolds.

Their attitude instructs the wise
that in this world, be wary
of all motion, strife and frenzy.

Man, made mad with shadow-chase,
bears, as punishment, the mark
of having wished to change his place.

FAT BLACK BIRD

They're renovating.
They're banging and building,
downtown
and in the suburbs.

And they're rushing,
from door to door,
office to office,
store to store.

And everywhere they go
they have telephones
attached to their faces.
Even in cars:

I saw one yesterday
behind tinted glass.
I couldn't tell
if it was a woman or a man
but I saw moving lips
and the flash of white plastic.

And it's not just the rich.
Last week I saw a labourer
in paint-smeared pants
walking briskly down Yonge Street —
he cradled a portable phone
close to his ear
as if it were a special pet.

I talk so seldom,
I almost envy them,
those with so much to say.
Or have I missed something?
I mean the emptiness

and all those voices
trying to scare it away
as if it were a fat black bird
that stands its ground
and is unflappable
and deaf.

CHAIR

It holds the light with a certain tension,
a concentration from being made, constrained,
the limitations of four legs, a bent-wood back
and the spare nomenclature — CHAIR.

When it is heavy with the weight
of a body, it assumes dignity;
in usage, solid,
unquestioning.

Alone, it invites other possibilities.
Take that painter of Provence
who each night
used it to hang his pants on.

In the morning light he saw it
as for the first time
and claimed it as a love subject
while the chair wondered if it was being transformed

or merely transferred
to a different set of perimeters:
that framed canvas, coloured
borders.

And you sit on it and talk
or read or gaze through the window
at leaves that shine
with their own intensity.

When they've cut the branches
who will see the trees for the leaves
luxurious beyond time, beyond
the trunk's brittle anxiety,

the four fleeing legs
of chair.

A BLACK BOOK

Burnt heart, seared letters whose serifs
almost touch

against a whiteness, a void expanse,
polar terror of the limitless.

Its creator departed, not missed,
an instrument whose gut once resounded

with the flux of his time, whose larynx flexed
against time — this, its deposit.

Once it threatened to swallow
the world it invented

but brought it back out of wreckage,
scarred, intact.

Between stiff covers, it scowls
with the scorn of the neglected

chords its empathy for the torn,
feeds off its dreams,

nurtures its rock, its frayed leaves
go on growing.

Postulates wholeness,
beginning and end,

but is strong in its knowledge
that this is illusion.

For some, a comfort
though not its intent

what it wishes now
more than to be read

is to wrestle each comer
down into its depths

into the blinding belly of its lastness.
Those who surface

are ash-eyed, born
from their breakage

whole image out of negative

dark fruition of the press.

TREASURE OF THE SIERRA MADRE

An unshaven foreigner
begs for quarters
in a small town
which is always on the border.

Hatch a scheme
or invent a plot:
three men, their pickaxes, canteens, canvas,
tin pans, suspicions, lust.

"No one gets the best of Fred C. Dobbs."
The paranoiac eyes of Bogart flare
in this desert fable
unfolding in *film noir*'s stark chiaroscuro.

Machetes, sombreros.
The maniacal bray of a burro.
The gold-capped laugh of a bandito.
The sneer when he says "Gringo."

Men dig their own graves.
Yet we too are driven by wants
and feel, even for pathetic thieves
as we hear the executioners' shots

and see the sad hats
being carried by wind
out to that wilderness
where gold mingles with dust.

TWO POEMS INSPIRED BY THE PRINTS OF GEORGE RAAB

i

Live Oaks in the Dead of Night

These trees give off
the bleeding shadows of Courbet
and the moon's biting light —
the mystical chiaroscuro
of French Pastoral.
                                        Your dream?

But this is the new country you have etched;
they only look like their distant cousins.
They're more like our original settlers, lonely, unowned,
who once drew from a moisture untouched
while at Chartres the water was already old
and metallic to the tongue.

Is all art dreaming backwards?
Your farm, with its barn, half housing horses,
half converted to a studio: presses, acids,
the thick richness of printmaker's paper,
your blue craftsman's apron —
another century's care and precision.

A country road, one of the last,
winds out of your garden
past a storybook silo, past
spotted cows from a children's primer

feeding eventually
into the unceasing, grinding, thoroughfare.

ii

Rhapsody in Milkweed

Dark stalks against the white expanse of snow.
Nature invents its own composition
for the artist to C —
that is, capture
by the trick
of reinventing it.

In the background,
tall pines are swept and obscured
by a blizzard. Is the rhapsody
the wind, a crazed flute
through the mountains?
Is the milkweed there to remind us
that when it bursts in late summer
and hovers in the air
we will dream of winter?

III

MAHABALIPURAM: DRAVIDIAN RUINS

Massive stone tigers and water buffaloes,
immovable, ochre with age;
yet in the unremitting sun they seem to eye me
as I move to touch shade.

At the temple's outer walls
I run my hand along reliefs:
fanned head of cobra,
smiling elephants, monkeys

their faces mournful or pitying;
humans with dog heads
and the bare-breasted goddesses linked to warrior lovers —
some myth I cannot connect

from an age when dreams could draw stories
from stone. Further on, I come upon
the living: a noseless leper
whose eyes are spaces, murmurs an incantation

as I pour a thin silver river
into his bandaged palms.
Beyond him are the hovels,
the shacks and the ocean

sounding furious, though its large statement
is reduced to surf. In the deep sand
my shoes, dark, cumbersome,
weigh like an accusation.

The beach line goes right and left
until the eye can see no farther.
Distance never hurts;
not like the particular:

the tuned hum of the waiting bus
with its silent, dissatisfied tourists;
the soiled white
of those outstretched bandages.

WHAT YOU SEE WHEN YOU ENTER BEIJING'S MUSEUM OF THE REVOLUTION

On the wall, a gigantic portrait of the uniformed Mao
and directly across from him, Marx and Engels:
two fierce, bearded, iconoclastic intellectuals
whose eyes are averted from those of the general.

POLAND

Poland is white and green
with its salt and forests.
And its kings are sunken into stone
with their drooping moustaches,
their swords and lost battles.

On the wooden table, the spilt vodka
has dried like a stain of blood
and in the churches
Miriam bends over her son
who has withered like a splint

while in the slow turgid river
that binds Crakow
gassed Hassids stare like fish
their lips pursed
without words.

THE VILLAGE

I visited the village my grandfather left
before the war. It was two hours
from Cracow
by car.

On the street the men, unshaven.
Some were too loud for midday
and tottered
when they walked.

Women peered out from doorways.
Scarves. Silver-capped teeth.
Inside the church,
candles burning,

a smear of gold and velvet
and the portrait of a blond, Slavic Jesus
while at the other end of the square —
the synagogue

untouched from the day the war ended,
its windows boarded,
its bricks resembled
discoloured salt.

Its presence was an absence
that settled inside of me.
I wanted to touch that community
once relegated to a ghetto

even if it were a community of ghosts
but when I ran my hand along the brick
what I felt
was lifeless, cold.

They say closeness to history
gives meaning
but I wondered if it isn't proximity
to death

feeling the absence
swell inside me,
knowing this to be a place
I might have been.

Chmielnick, Poland. 1988

THE CEMETERY

The sign over the cemetery read:

No dumping garbage.
This is sacred ground.

And indeed the area was green
with no garbage.

But over the years
the townsfolk had stolen the headstones.

From the hill I was on
I looked down at the narrow streets,
at the unattractive post-war houses
and wondered what veranda or step
had my ancestors' name on it
turned downward,
toward the dark.

They had left one stone.
It was chipped and cracked.
It leaned at a 45 degree angle
like a silent film comedian
about to fall back on his head.

Why leave one, I wondered.

You could no longer make out the Hebrew letters.
They had, for the most part, vanished
leaving only faint, mysterious traces
in the silent stone.

Chmielnick, Poland. 1988

WARSAW

The moon, a Slavic skull,
shines over Warsaw

and on the crowded Jewish cemetery,
that final ghetto
of touching stones,
chiselled hieroglyphs
which should be breath vowels,
gutturals against death
but there is no one
to intone them.

In Warsaw at night
you discover the Absence.
Too many armies
have stomped on its streets,
its buildings
seem to be sinking,
each human face
folds in beneath lamplight
like a crater.

The soles of people's shoes
are ugly and thick
as if shoemakers had become philosophers
of pavement.

The people have lost
their lightness
and replaced it with a wisdom
which makes no one laugh.

CITIES

Travelling, one accepts everything.
— Elias Canetti (*The Voices of Marrakesh*)

1. PARIS, 1969 (for Samiha Abdel Sayed)

From my balcony on the Boulevard St. Michel
I watched blue-peaked gendarmes chase the student rebels.
Chilled wine, café days. "Have you read Chomsky?"
The New Left plugged the journals; in Luxembourg Gardens
Dylan blared. *Culture?* I marched
past centuries of oil at the Louvre
but stopped dead at the Jeu de Pomme's shock of colour.
My concierge in pink rollers seemed always to be sitting
under a portable hair-drier reading translated
Raymond Chandler. Glad I was from a country half-French
she said she despised Americans.
Security's sub-machine guns escorted us to the waiting
El-Al jet. Already I could taste the tension of Tel Aviv.
The Valéry in my carry-on seemed otherworldly, thin.

2. VENICE

What was Wilde's quip? "A gondola in Venice —
like riding a trash can through a sewer."
But even the photo-snapping tourists in Piazza San Marco
could not detract from the awesome grandeur.
A city whose central tension is between stone and water.
Reconstruction everywhere: scaffolds,
curators and yes, Wilde, the odour.
Newly married, I recall nights of oil black canals,
lemon veal, tartufo. We stained the thick
starched sheets of our second-class hotel.
In the old Jewish ghetto we purchased an ancient world map
ringed with sea creatures, gods, naive emblems of the zodiac.
Seeing us, the shopwoman cried in amazement, "So young!"
We walked in silence, holding her words like a talisman.

3. FLORENCE

Manly city, once stoical and spare, whose great sculptors
all were bachelors. Here, the dialectical eye
moves from mustard, buff, pale yellow, cream
to the black and white marble of the Baptistery,
the deep green and flashing gold of San Miniato.
Stone worn by time into grandeur is onerous;
it weighs upon the populace who try to fly
on mopeds or in dark Fiats
beneath the bald eyes and open book of their Poet
who consigns them to his newest circle — Sameness.
Transvestites strut outside the American Express Office.
On Ponte Vecchio I haggled for trinkets and thought
of Michelangelo who himself climbed the Tuscan hills
to split stone and load the panting asses.

4. CHIANGMAI

On the streets, women still unashamed enough
to spontaneously do The Fingernail Dance — finger blades
flash like fans, eyes riveted,
the tentative bird steps. There,
and in the murky stalls where silversmiths
hammer on anvils the bowls with brutal dragons,
pendants scratched with emblems of Chance —
I saw the old Orient, that compromise
between what one is born into
and what one can shape with one's hands.
North of the city, a visit to the hill tribes of Old Siam
— man without his making —
huts, lice, the running sores of children.
They asked if we carried medicine.

5. XIAN

At the city's borders
are the vacant plundered tombs of ancient emperors.
I watched police direct young dissidents in black workpants
each carrying shovel or pickaxe — about to be "re-educated."
What they were unearthing was the Terra-Cotta Army:
line after line of fierce bearded men
whose sole purpose had been their ruler's protection.
You might view them as examples of grand craftsmanship
(the guide book claims each figure is somewhat different)
or an obsessive's plodding attempt to undo death.
The dust from the digging dried out my throat.
Later in the streets, I stared at row after row
of faces: thin, disillusioned; ascetic blue jackets —
the living legions.

6. SAIGON, 1973

(*from* David Jenkins' *Asia on the Cheap*)

"The best place in Saigon to go for a drink is the terrace
of the old four-storey Continental Palace. Sit for hours
and watch the wide faces of Vietnamese girls,
their phoenix eyes, their hair a midnight blue-black sea.
They seem to float. Their tissue-thin silken dresses,
slit up the side, may catch a light breeze.
Shoeshine boys with hawk eyes move from table to table
nod knowingly at each pair of heavy black boots.
Bombs may start falling at dusk. A distant rumble
then the steady crump, crump, crump
as the B52s disgorge their load.
Open-fronted shops sell big lacquered elephants
with symbols for Prosperity, Longevity
and Happiness. Admirable things to wish for in Vietnam."

7. AKKO

Mediterranean city known for conquests and death.
Cannons still face the sea that glints like a scimitar,
that roars with the chilling jubilance of Turkish invaders.
And the fortress on that shore calcified with sea-salt and
sun,
so white it seems composed of bones.
In a diner, far from my battle of the generations,
I watched two men I imagined were father and son
poised over a game of backgammon
and wondered if distance alters anything.
In the window, a lamb's inverted torso
drew a chorus of fanatic flies,
the room expectant with the sinister
undercurrent of gurgling hookahs,
the punctuated clack of worry beads and dice.

8. JERUSALEM

(for Michael and Anita Greenstein)

From Mount of Olives, the gold Dome of the Rock
reflects a sun so intense I can see the blade of Abraham,
hear Mohammed's horse's hooves claw an arid heaven.
In the Arab market, a pyramid of sheep's heads —
the startled congregation. Here, the archeologist's job
is permanent for below this city is another,
and below that another as if there were no end to history
which if you succeed in unravelling, is God's voice
with its perfect conundrum: "I am who I am,"
sending you back to man. At each station of the cross,
no matter how much banter, you can hear a nail drop.
At the temple wall the pressing intonations out of
the diasporic wind: trials, questions, lamentations.
Beneath my hand the ochre stone turns to skin.

9. HIROSHIMA

In Peace Park Museum, bins of melted
Hirohito glasses, scorched fabric, bone bits
and the wall of stopped clocks: 8:15.
And 8:15 again. I walked
amongst the unnatural newness
of white buildings, the sun seemed to be burning
through an unclean filter,
the air crackled with the sound of Geiger counters —
I believed I was breathing the contagion of death.
Even the U.S. servicemen were solemn,
eyes fastened to the pavement
where every other block you might stumble on a marker,
a small stone that reads:
School children vanished here.

10. KYOTO

(for John Oughton)

In Nara Park, the cold black nose of a Disney-like doe,
her soft tongue like felt on my feeding palm.
Kimonos. Silence. A picture book of old Japan.
In the Imperial Gardens the platoon of reverent pruners
leaves nothing untouched — here the paradisial is always
artificial. At Madame Ono's youth hostel, German students
train to be Kerouac Buddhists. And the grim Californian
who uses Nietzsche for a pillow.
The incessant machinery of Tokyo seems so far away
even the doll-house tea ceremony is not laughable.
A clear bell at each temple and clear Kyoto water
in a dragon-mouthed ladle.
I am infinitesimal but also reaching the furthest shore
as I muse upon the rock garden's concentric circles.

11. MADRAS

On a scalding pavement, blotches of betel juice
like blood drops trailing from a victim.
Downtown traffic clotted by a procession of smiling
elephants.
In this city the head is rearranged by the sun
and the gaping contradictions: a pink palace
rising out of a slum; a white lotus shimmering
in cow dung. Green Bengali sweets in glistening foil
and the vacant eyes of beggars, the dust of wasted soil.
At the old British Fort there are no such opposites
to disorient the traveller: calm-faced generals
and governors gaze out from gilded frames;
their wives shine like porcelain.
And locked in glass cabinets:
log-books, stamps, seals, sabres.

12. AGRA (Taj Mahal)

A rickshaw through Agra's saffron dawn.
Early market: vendors squat and spit,
the smoke of harsh *beedees* mixes with the fragrance
of cardamom, turmeric. Boys hawk trinkets
on the path to the monument that opposes life's flux:
white marble born out of hurt flesh, grief's darkness,
tomb of a delicate princess, her beauty translated
into latticework and minarets, so dreamlike they seem
to question their existence, promising to levitate
and join the cumulous jet. The semi-precious inlay
swirls like mock scripture — eye language;
the rectangular pool before it, cool carpet of water
with its oriental lesson of mirrors
reflecting what is changing, what is changeless.

13. BENARES

Wailing women. A father's body
turns to black diamond then collapses to ash,
sifted into the Ganges with a flurry of white lotus.
Here, the soul is burned to last. Orange garlands,
clasped hands, the third eye, flame-coloured and central.
Naked Saddhus draw water up through nostrils,
throat, even rectum, reminding us
that all discipline is a form of purification.
No matter what time of day, time seems frozen:
the heart's standstill, the fluttering will.
A whole city built on a river
for the sole benefit of the soul's departure.
Whoever is brought here is bound, to return again.
In the blue flames mourners meet their reflections.

14. BOMBAY

(for Christopher Levenson)

Music and decay. At the Elephanta Caves
great rock sculptures loom like a who's who
of Hindu deities: Shiva, Vishnu, Garuda, Saraswati.
Chipped, with flattened noses and eroded ears
they resemble the lepers drawing tourists' coins
with their stumps of crusted fingers.
Winged black notes clot the blue Bombay air.
On Malabar I can connect: Hanging Gardens
and the Towers of Silence atop which bodies of Parsis
feed birds of prey — a clean vanishing.
Each night a wake for a street kid gone under:
South Indian drums and a quivering, climbing vocal
sends the soul on its looped journey —
in the choral darkness, a shower of white petals.

15. KANDY

A full moon, the fluorescence of enamel.
I awake to sudden shadows on the wall —
the torch procession of a lunar ritual: tambourines,
drums, horns that sound like chased geese;
smell of incense, cloves; the flash of sarongs, batik.
An elephant in jewelled caparison with enormous tusks
carries the tiny tooth of a sage set in gold lotus.
Buddha's temple is candy-floss pink,
throngs with his devotees. Here they feel whole
like the complete globe of his paunch
which taught abstinence. The nighttime mirror
of the city's small lake makes me believe
in the substance of nothing. My hand
in moonlight is a white fish. Breathing is a dream.

16. COLOMBO

Thin dark wraiths in white sarongs
mop the floor under the gaze of the manager
who reminds them he's a burgher. Colonial soul.
At the city limits there's the jungle
but the city itself is a jungle: lineups for food,
armed troops, the smoked glass of a BMW.
A barefoot Singhalese, fakir's needle through his cheeks,
shakes a can of change in my face —
the desperate theatre of begging.
Each morning I walk past birds in a cage,
their wings the shade of avocado. The evening sun is heavy
like an overripe mango. A sultry beauty, then dusk.
Leaves of the palm trees appear to be the outstretched
arms
of pleading women before being swallowed by darkness.

17. KIEV, 1988

The onion domes, turquoise and gold of Eastern orthodoxy.
Here the People themselves are a Christ so long underground
he's forgotten his name. Ukrainian wheat fields
tug at the city's memory, but in government buildings
the soul blanks at the shuffle of footsteps
the soporific scratch of a pen. In the national museum
I stood before Cossacks, their dagger moustaches
and stallion eyes and found no resemblances
in the queues for bread and cheese, nor in the sulking KGB
openly touring my hotel lobby. Obvious bugs
hung from my ceiling like resigned water sprinklers —
where was the fire?
Gorbachov was prying open Stalin's fist.
Empty store windows shone like the eyes of dazed
amnesiacs.

18. LENINGRAD, 1988

The Neva's railings spouted sea-gods and anchors.
The Fortress of Peter and Paul's spire
jabbed like a hypodermic into the northern blue absence.
At the Admiralty I could see what Mandelstam had meant
by the fierce carpenter's eye as opposed to the whim
of inspiration. I swallowed his *Kamen*
and recalled his covenant with tar,
with voices of the dead
(he'd memorized their telephone numbers)
while awaiting the trench coats, those "dear guests."
June's white nights made for shallow sleep
as if someone had left a bald bulb burning.
I walked and walked imagining a man in exile.
Lineups everywhere for books and sandals.

19. HALIFAX

(for Andy Wainwright and Marjorie Stone)

In the narrow harbour streets
I can envision the garrison captains, their bonneted wives,
epaulets and lace, guardians of trade, this touchstone
of Britain. When my friend describes the 1917 explosion
I see the flash, shards shower over the iron Atlantic —
a collision of foreign ships. On shore: 1600 dead,
9000 wounded, 200 blinded.
Dimness bled inland — a people of impaired vision.
Now hands sing in the dark and the harbour is a mouth
feeding the commercial heart beating westward.
The houses here are wooden-framed, well-maintained,
some aspire to colour. But in the populated, fluorescent mall
we walk from shop to familiar shop
and I believe I am back in Toronto.

20. TORONTO

Up close hardly anything's exotic.
Undramatic city of my childhood,
swallowed by banks, towers, chic streets,
boutiques — most admired city on the continent
according to Gallup. But in summer,
on the islands, you can feel the age-old swamp:
the bone-tightening dampness off Lake Ontario
with its indestructible frontier mosquitoes
not even industry could kill.
No matter how many ethnics or how much
glitz, the grey parliamentary heart of Queen's Park lives;
no matter what party's in power, it always seems
conservative. The road pattern forms a logical grid.
Staid and sure. Ravine green.
A good place for departures and returns.

Also by Kenneth Sherman:

Snake Music
The Cost of Living
Words for Elephant Man
Black Flamingo
Relations (editor)
The Book of Salt
Jackson's Point